Y0-CZO-428

# Old Testament Friends
## Men of Courage

**ROBERT G. FULBRIGHT**

ILLUSTRATED BY **BILL McPHEETERS**

**BROADMAN PRESS**
Nashville, Tennessee

# Contents

4

# Noah Listened to God

When God created the world, he also created Adam and Eve. Adam and Eve had disobeyed God and sinned. Their children and grandchildren also sinned. People became so wicked that God was sorry he had created them. Because the people were wicked, God decided to destroy them by sending a great flood.

There was one good man living. This man was Noah. Noah loved God. He tried to do everything he could to please God.

One day God told Noah to build a big boat (ark).

Because Noah loved and believed God, he did exactly as God told him. Noah and his three sons began work. They worked

for many years building this big boat. Noah knew God would send a flood.

As Noah worked on the boat, he told the other people about God's warning. They only laughed at Noah and his family for building this strange-looking boat on dry land.

Then one day the boat was finished. God told Noah to take his wife, his three sons and their wives, and get in the boat. Then God sent pairs of every kind of animal and bird on the earth to the boat. They were all put on the boat. This was a part of God's plan to save the things he had made.

When Noah's family and the animals

were in the boat, God closed the door. Noah and his family waited for seven days before the rains began.

The rains poured down. It rained for forty days and nights. Soon all the land was covered with water. The only living people now were in the boat. God saved Noah and his family. They were safe inside the ark where God protected them.

The water stayed on the earth for many days. Noah and his family waited inside the ark.

Then God made the winds to blow. The waters began to disappear. One day Noah sent out a raven. But it never returned. Later he sent out a dove, but it came back. A week later Noah sent out the dove again.

It returned with a leaf in its beak. Noah
knew then the flood was over so he and his
family and all the animals left the ark.

Noah was glad to see the green earth
again. Immediately he built an altar and
worshiped God.

God was pleased with Noah and his sons.
"I am going to make a promise to you,"
God said to Noah, "and this promise is to
all people who live after you." Then God
promised he would never destroy the
world again with a flood. Noah and his

family knew God would keep his promise. This made them very glad. "I will put a rainbow in the sky for everyone to see. This rainbow will remind people of my promise," God said.

**Thinkback:** Why did God send the flood? Who stayed in the ark during the flood?

What promise did God make after the flood? What is a reminder of that promise that we can see today?

## Isaac Was a Man of Peace

Many years ago, God made a promise to Abraham. That promise is sometimes called a covenant. God promised Abraham that he would become great. God told Abraham that his family would number as many as the stars in the sky.

When Abraham was ninety-nine years old, and Sarah was nearly that old, they had a son. They named him Isaac. Abraham and Sarah were happy with Isaac and thanked God for him.

Isaac grew to be a fine boy. He was obedient to his parents. As he grew to be a man, Abraham shared with him God's promise or covenant. God could now carry out that promise through Isaac and his children.

11

The years passed, and Isaac grew to be a
man. Abraham and Sarah became very
old, and finally Sarah died. Abraham and
Isaac were lonely without her.

Abraham spoke to one of his most
trusted servants: "I want you to go to
Haran and find a wife for Isaac.

The servant prayed and asked God for help. He then took ten camels and many gifts on his journey to Haran. After many days of traveling, he reached the well outside the city of Haran. Young girls were coming out to the well for water.

The servant had asked God to let the right girl get water for him and offer to get some water for his camels.

A young woman named Rebekah was at the well. "Give me a drink of water," the servant said to her.

"I will," she answered, "and I will also water your camels." The servant was happy. He knew he had found the right girl to be Isaac's wife.

Early the next day, Rebekah said good-bye to her family. Rebekah went with the servant to Abraham's home. There she became Isaac's wife.

Isaac and Rebekah asked God to give them children. Finally twin boys were born. They named the twins Jacob and Esau.

Later a severe famine came over the land. It became hot and dry. There was not enough food and water for the sheep and cattle.

Isaac thought, "I must move to Egypt." But God told Isaac to stay in Gerar. "I will bless you," God said. "This is the land I have promised you."

Isaac loved God and stayed in Gerar. He dug new wells. He had enough water. His crops grew.

The people of Gerar did not like Isaac. They filled Isaac's wells with dirt. This made Isaac angry. "We must not fight," he said. "Dig the wells again," he told his men.

King Abimelech came to Isaac and said, "These wells are on our land. You must move off our land." Isaac was a kind man. He did not want to fight. Isaac moved his family and animals to another place in Gerar.

Isaac had to dig new wells. God helped Isaac. He and his family had plenty of water.

King Abimelech wanted these new wells also. The king told Isaac that he was too rich. He told Isaac to move to another land.

Isaac moved his family again. This time they moved far away. They had to dig new wells.

One day King Abimelech and three men came to Isaac. "God is with you and protects you," they said. "We will not bother you again. We want to be friends."

Isaac had a party for the king and his new friends. There was peace in the land and every one was happy.

**Thinkback:** What is another word for *promise?* What promise did God make to Abraham and Isaac?

What were the names of Isaac and Rebekah's twins?

# Jacob Knew God's Love

Rebekah and Isaac had twins, Esau and Jacob. The twins did not look alike. They were also different in other ways.

Jacob liked to be with his mother and help her. He stayed near the home. Esau was a good hunter, and he liked the outdoors. He often did things that pleased his father.

17

Esau was born first. By family law, he was to be the head of the family when Isaac died. It was God's plan for Jacob to be head of this family. Jacob was selfish and wanted the birthright and his father's blessing. So he and his mother, Rebekah, played a trick to get it. Jacob was not willing to wait for God to work things out.

Isaac was now old and almost blind. He was ready to give his blessing to Esau. He called Esau and said: "Go hunting and bring me a deer. Cook it the way I like it. We will talk, and I will give the blessing that is yours as the firstborn son."

Rebekah overheard what Isaac had told Esau. Quickly she went to find Jacob. She told him to go kill two little goats from the flock. She would cook them like deer meat.

18

Tricky Jacob took advantage of Esau and Isaac. Jacob took the cooked meat to his father. Jacob covered his arms with animal skins so that to his blind father he would feel like Esau. So Isaac gave the blessing to Jacob, thinking he was Esau.

When Esau returned from hunting, he learned what Jacob had done. Esau became terribly angry. He threatened to kill Jacob.

Jacob quickly left home. He went to the faraway land of Haran.

As he traveled on his way, he thought of the trouble he had brought upon himself. He wondered if he would ever see his parents again.

19

That night when Jacob slept, God sent
him a wonderful dream. In his dream,
Jacob saw a ladder. It reached from earth
to heaven. He saw angels going up and
down the ladder. God said to Jacob: "I am
the Lord, the God of Abraham and Isaac, I
will give to you and to your descendants
this land on which you are lying. They will
be as numerous as the specks of dust on the

20

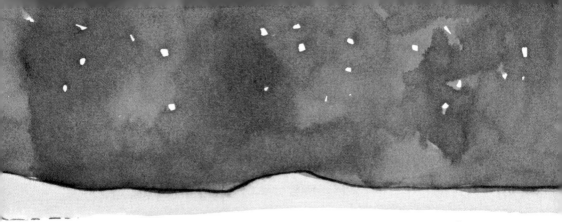

earth. They will extend their territory in all directions, and through you and your descendants I will bless all the nations. Remember, I will be with you and protect you wherever you go, and I will bring you back to this land. I will not leave you until I have done all that I have promised you" (Genesis 28:13-15, TEV). This was the same promise (covenant) that God had given Abraham and Isaac.

Early the next morning, Jacob took a stone and set it up as an altar. He named the place *Bethel* which means "house of God." Jacob then knew that God would always care for him.

Jacob lived in Haran for twenty years. He married and had a family. But he knew he had done wrong. He wanted to return home. At last, he decided to leave Haran. He wanted to make peace with his brother.

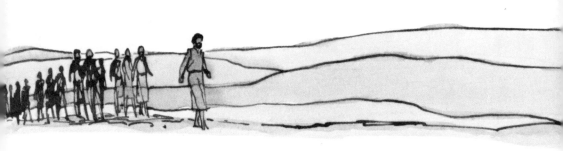

Jacob often thought of the time he had lied to his father. He also remembered the time he had tricked Esau. Jacob was sorry he had done wrong.

He must return home even though he did not know what Esau would do to him. Jacob started the long trip home. With his family, he took large flocks and herds. He sent a messenger to tell Esau he was returning home.

The messenger returned and told Jacob that Esau was coming to meet him with four hundred men! Jacob was afraid. He sent Esau some of the animals from his flocks. Jacob asked God to help him. He prayed, "Save me from the anger of my brother, for I am afraid of him."

The night before Jacob met Esau, another strange thing happened. God sent

an angel to Jacob. They wrestled all night.
Jacob asked the angel to bless him.

"Your name shall no longer be Jacob,
but Israel," the angel said, "for God has
changed your life."

Jacob saw Esau coming in the distance.
When he reached him, Jacob bowed
before him in a humble way seven times.
Esau rushed to put his arms around Jacob.
He was forgiven!

Jacob was now back home in the land which God had promised him.

**Thinkback:** What were some wrong things Jacob did to Esau? Was Jacob sorry for the wrong he had done? How did he know that Esau forgave him?

HARAN

NINEVEH

SUSA

BABYLON

SHUNEM
DAMASCUS

MT. TABOR
MT. CARMEL

DOTHAN
BETHEL
ANATHOTH
JERUSALEM
TIMNAH
BETHLEHEM
GAZA

JERICHO
JOPPA
GILGAL

MT. NEBO

GERAR
MORESHETH
HEBRON
TEKOA

EGYPT

# SOME OLD TESTAMENT PLACES

26

# Joshua and Caleb Were Faithful

For many years, the children of Israel had been slaves in Egypt. Then God chose Moses to lead them back to Canaan—the Promised Land. God had promised this land to the children of Israel many years before.

The trip from Egypt to Canaan was a long one. The people complained. They disappointed God many times. Because of this, God made the trip even harder. All along the way, God did many wonderful things. He gave them food. He provided a pillar of cloud by day and a pillar of fire by night to lead them. He gave them water. Still the people complained.

After years of traveling, they came right to the border of Canaan. Even though this was the land God had promised them, there were people living there. There were large cities with high walls built around them.

God told Moses to select some men to go over into Canaan and see what it was like. They were to go in as spies.

Moses chose twelve men to go. He told the twelve what to look for. He told them to see what kind of land they found, and what food could be grown. He also told them to see what kind of people were living there and what kind of cities were built.

Quietly the twelve spies slipped into Canaan. They looked all around the country for forty days. They remembered all that Moses had told them. When they returned, they brought a cluster of grapes so large it had to be carried on a pole between two men.

29

All the people gathered to hear the report. The spies began telling about how wonderful the land was. "The land is as good as God said it would be," the men said. "But we could never capture the cities. We are afraid."

Then Caleb, one of the spies and a man of courage, spoke up. "The land is wonderful. It is as God has promised. And with God's help, I know we can take it. Let's get ready and go at once." Only Joshua agreed with Caleb. The other spies were all afraid.

The report made the people scared. They were afraid they could not take the land. They complained all night to Moses.

Joshua and Caleb were men of courage. They did all they could to persuade the people to go into the land God had

30

promised them. The people became so angry they wanted to kill Joshua and Caleb.

God was disappointed again with the people. He would not let the people go unpunished. God told the people that all who were over twenty years of age would not go into the Promised Land. They would stay in the wilderness another forty years. Of the adults then living, only Joshua and Caleb would live to enter the land of Canaan. They were men of courage who had been faithful spies.

Moses had been a good leader. He always tried to encourage the people to obey God and God's laws. Now Moses was getting old and would not be able to go into the Promised Land. He was 120 years old. He had led God's people from Egypt up to

the land that God had promised them.
Now God would choose a younger man to
be the leader. The new leader would help
capture Canaan.

Moses called the people together. He
reminded them of all that God had done
for them. He urged them to obey God. He
told them to teach their children about
God and to keep his Commandments.
Moses then sang a farewell song.

Moses then laid his hands on the new leader God had chosen. The new leader was a man of courage—Joshua!

Moses climbed to the top of Mount Nebo where he could see the Promised Land. While on the mountaintop with God, Moses died.

Joshua would now lead the people into the Promised Land.

**Thinkback:** Why were spies sent into Canaan? What report did the spies bring back?

How did Joshua and Caleb differ from the other spies?

What new leader did God choose when Moses died?

# Ezra Taught God's Law

For many years, the Jewish people were slaves in Babylon. Then a kind man named Cyrus became king of Babylon. He permitted the people to return to Jerusalem and Judah. Some of the Jews stayed in Babylon while others returned to Jerusalem.

The Temple in Jerusalem and much of the city had been destroyed. Zerubbabel had led the people to rebuild the Temple. The city was very poor. The walls had crumbled and broken. Thieves could easily get in.

Word began to spread about the hard times the Jews were having in Jerusalem. This word reached Ezra. Ezra was a prophet still living in Babylon. Ezra loved God very much. He spent time every day reading and studying God's Word. Ezra had spent much time searching for the books of the Law. As he found the books, he copied them, putting them together in one book. This book had in it the writings of Moses, Judges, Kings, and the prophets.

Ezra studied these books until he knew them well. Then Ezra started a school where he could teach other men about God's word. These men were called scribes, and they made copies of the Law from Ezra's book.

One day Ezra heard about the poor
people in Jerusalem. He had no money he
could send. But he could go and teach
them about God. If they learned about
God's law and obeyed it, God would help
them have the other things they needed.

Ezra made the long trip from Babylon to
Jerusalem. When the people heard he was
coming, they were happy. They planned a
special service for the study of God's Law.

A platform was built in the city square. It
was near one of the important gates of the
city. Levites, who were helpers, were
chosen to work with Ezra. They would
explain the words in the Bible scrolls.

The people all gathered around the platform. What an exciting day it was! Ezra walked up on the platform. Everyone became very quiet and still. Each person wanted to hear every word Ezra said. Before he began to read the Law, he said, "Blessed be the Lord, the great God."

The people answered, "Amen, Amen." They bowed their heads. They loved God very much. They were grateful for Ezra who could teach them more about God.

Then Ezra began reading the scroll. Everyone listened. When they heard the words of the Law, they knew they had done wrong. They began to cry. They knew they had not obeyed God's laws.

Ezra talked to the people. "Do not cry," he said, "for God forgives you. This is a day for rejoicing. Go home and prepare some food. Share it with someone who does not have as much as you do."

The people did as Ezra said. It was a great day of feasting.

The next day, the people all gathered to hear Ezra again. When Ezra went to the platform, he told them to observe the Feast of Booths, as the book of the Law commanded.

Each family was to build a booth on the housetop, in the courtyard or street, or in the court of the Temple. They were to gather branches of leaves from palm trees, olive trees, myrtle trees, or other leafy trees to make the booths. For seven days the people were to live in the booths. While in the booths, they must have looked around and thanked God for all he had done. And every day they went to hear Ezra and the scribes read more from the book of Law.

Finally, on the eighth day, the people gathered again to worship. This was a special worship service. At this worship service, the people promised God they would keep his laws.

Ezra was a courageous leader. He helped the people of Jerusalem know about God.

**Thinkback:** What have you learned about Ezra? What did he do in Babylon and in Jerusalem?

What is the Feast of Booths?

# Nehemiah Helped His People

Nehemiah lived far away from Judah, his homeland. He lived in Persia. Nehemiah had a very important job. He worked for the king of Persia. He had an office in the palace. Nehemiah was the cupbearer for the king. This meant that he tasted the king's food and wine before the king ate and drank it. Nehemiah did this to see that no one had poisoned the food. Because of this, the king trusted Nehemiah.

One day a friend brought sad news to Nehemiah. "Jerusalem is in very bad condition. You would be very sad to see it. The walls and gates are torn down. The people are not safe. Robbers come at night and steal."

This news made Nehemiah sad. He wondered how he could help.

When Nehemiah served the king his dinner that night, the king saw that Nehemiah was sad. "Why do you look so sad, Nehemiah?" the king asked.

Then Nehemiah told the king the bad news about Jerusalem. He told the king about how the walls had been torn down and the gates burned.

The king listened carefully. He wanted to help so he asked, "Is there some way I can help you?"

Nehemiah asked the king if he could go back to Jerusalem to help rebuild the walls. The king agreed to let Nehemiah go to Jerusalem. The king also gave him letters to the rulers of the countries through which Nehemiah would travel. The king gave him permission to cut wood from the king's forest to make the gates and walls strong.

44

Nehemiah began the long journey from Persia back to Judah. When he arrived, he saw the torn-down walls. There were heaps of stones and ashes where the strong walls once stood. Rubbish was piled high.

The next day Nehemiah went to the priests and rulers of the city. He talked to them about the trouble the city was in. Nehemiah told the people of his plan to rebuild the walls. The people listened to Nehemiah. They were pleased he had come to help. Everyone wanted to help. They worked very hard. Even some of the women helped build the wall.

The enemies of Jerusalem became very angry. They tried to get the workers to stop building the wall. The Samaritans, who were the enemies, did not want to see Jerusalem become a strong city again. If it did, they could no longer rob and steal. They tried to make trouble for the Jews.

Nehemiah and his workers kept right on rebuilding the wall. Nehemiah said to the Samaritans, "God is going to help us with our work, and surely he will punish you."

When the Samaritans saw that the Jews were going to rebuild the wall, they called on other nations to help them stop the Jews. But the Jews prayed to God for help. Nehemiah then divided the workers so that part of them guarded the wall with spears and swords while the others worked.

God was with his people. He helped Nehemiah know what to do. The walls and gates were finished. Jerusalem became a strong city once again.

Nehemiah stayed in Jerusalem for a while after the walls were completed. He was then governor of Jerusalem.

**Thinkback:** What was Nehemiah's job in the palace?
Why was Nehemiah sad?

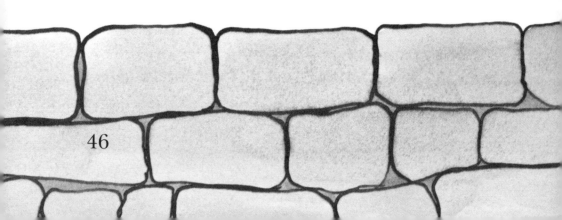

How did the king of Persia help
Nehemiah and Jerusalem?
What were two things Nehemiah did in
Jerusalem?

17

# Reflections

- Of these seven Bible persons, which one do you like best? Why?
- Can you recall one thing about each Bible person that made him a man of courage?
- Recall at least one time when each of these men prayed to God. Did God answer these prayers?

Are you ever afraid? Do you not know what to do in certain situations? Are there hard decisions you have to make? If so, consider . . .

- talking to God.
- thinking about people of courage who looked to God for help.
- finding a friend with whom you can share.

Remember, these Bible friends were not perfect. Each was once a child like you. God used him. God can use you. Each wanted to please God.

How can you please God?